1

1. Introduction

From mid-2007 until early 2009, central banks extended the equivalent of about $4 trillion in major currencies in liquidity support to banks and non-banks, to individual institutions and markets, and in domestic and foreign currency. As a consequence of these actions, the aggregate size of central bank balance sheets in major currency areas more than doubled. Subsequently, until mid-2010, central banks wound down this liquidity support, but even so balance sheets continued to expand because of asset purchase programmes and, in the euro area, new support measures in response to the sovereign debt crisis.

During the financial crisis, central banks accumulated a vast amount of experience in the execution of the lender of last resort role. This contrasts sharply with the post-Second World War period, when emergency liquidity support had been provided rarely and almost always to individual banking institutions experiencing idiosyncratic and usually transitory difficulties. In a number of cases, central banks had not provided emergency liquidity support for decades.

The crisis experience has challenged commonly held views on how central banks should provide emergency liquidity support. The most widely held were those put forward by Walter Bagehot in his book "Lombard Street" – to stem a financial panic a central bank should lend freely at a penalty rate to solvent institutions against good collateral (Bagehot (1873)). By lending freely, the central bank could prevent a financial crisis and the associated fire sales of assets and disruptions to economic activity. But by lending at a penalty rate to solvent institutions against good collateral, the central bank avoided taking unnecessary risks and reduced moral hazard.

Another widely held view was that ex ante ambiguity about the provision of liquidity support can effectively contain moral hazard. "Constructive ambiguity" was a central piece of lender of last resort policies of many central banks before the crisis. Obviously, such ambiguity did not prevent the build-up of excessive maturity and currency mismatches in the global financial system. Nor is it clear how credible constructive ambiguity is now in light of the crisis experience of large-scale liquidity support.

In this paper, we review the various ways that central banks provided emergency liquidity assistance (ELA) during the crisis, and we discuss issues for the design of ELA arising from that experience. We try to show how the rules which governed central banks' provision of ELA during the financial crisis differed from those governing ELA pre-crisis. We do not judge the appropriateness of ELA provided during the crisis. Views differ on this issue,[5] and we do not take a stand on this debate in our paper.

In many ways, the emergency liquidity support since 2007 has largely adhered to Bagehot's dictum of lending freely at a penalty rate to solvent institutions against good collateral. Even as the crisis became systemic, central banks aimed at acting in the spirit of Bagehot by taking decisive action to stem the crisis while avoiding unnecessary risks for central banks. As we will discuss, these were the situations where the lender of last resort role of central banks was most difficult.

---

[5] Carlson et al (2014) includes a discussion of the varying views on the effectiveness and appropriateness of lender of last resort lending during the crisis.

Following Freixas et al (1999), we define the lender of last resort as the institution that provides liquidity to an individual financial institution (or the market as a whole) in reaction to an abnormal increase in demand for liquidity that cannot be met from an alternative source. Lender of last resort credit in these situations is often referred to as emergency liquidity assistance. In the standard conception of such lending, the financial institution in question would be solvent but illiquid; that is, its assets are more valuable than its liabilities, but it is unable to raise funds to meet short-term obligations. Last resort lending in these circumstances would prevent a costly and unnecessary default by the institution.

In the next section, we briefly survey the views on emergency liquidity assistance held by economists and central bankers going into the crisis. The third section provides a summary of the various ways that central banks provided ELA in 2007–10 and infers the rules that appear to have governed its provision. The fourth section discusses issues in the future provision of ELA to markets and institutions.

2. Pre-crisis views on the lender of last resort role

The role of lender of last resort is probably the most ambiguous function of a central bank. On the one hand, it is typically regarded as a core responsibility of central banks, given their unique ability to create liquid assets in the form of central bank reserves, their central position within the payment system and their macroeconomic stabilisation objective. On the other hand, if the availability of central bank liquidity were certain, individual banks would have reduced incentives to maintain sufficient stocks of liquid assets to cover their liquidity needs. Hence, to limit moral hazard, central banks have in many cases left open how they would respond to liquidity shortages at the level of individual institutions or the market as a whole.

Pre-crisis views on ELA reflect this inherent tension between the recognition that central bank liquidity support is unavoidable in certain situations and concerns about moral hazard. This section summarises the views in the literature and central bank approaches towards ELA.

2.1 Views in the literature

Freixas et al (1999) provide a comprehensive review of the literature on ELA, covering the need for ELA, central banks' responses to illiquidity problems via liquidity support to individual institutions and via lending to the market as a whole, and the costs of and moral hazard due to ELA.[6]

Reasons for providing ELA. The main reason identified by Freixas et al (1999) for ELA to individual banks is to avoid a solvent bank becoming illiquid because of inefficiencies in the interbank market, which may prevent such a bank from borrowing from other banks. The need for liquidity support arises from the existence of asymmetric information, which can lead to bank runs and a failure of interbank

---

[6] Freixas et al (1999) also discuss risk-capital support for insolvent banks and the costs of capital injections.

markets; and negative externalities for systemic financial stability from the failure of a bank, due to contagion and interbank credit exposures.

ELA can also help to prevent contagion. Such contagion could occur for two primary reasons. First, an institution that had lent money to the defaulter could become insolvent because of losses on the defaulted obligations. Second, an institution could be viewed as having similar portfolios to the defaulting institution, and worried creditors could stop funding it. In either case, if an institution is unable to raise funds and is forced to sell assets at fire-sale prices, those lower asset values can push it and other institutions into insolvency. ELA can prevent unnecessary fire sales by providing liquidity to otherwise solvent institutions. For instance, the Federal Reserve took a number of steps to increase the liquidity available to financial institutions after the stock market crash of 1987 (Greenspan (1988), Carlson (2007)).[7]

Finally, ELA can also prevent a disorderly bankruptcy, which can in turn have disruptive effects on the wider financial system. It can do so either by enabling a solvent but illiquid bank to weather a transitory withdrawal of market funding, or by allowing financial authorities time to arrange an orderly failure.

Costs from providing ELA. One cost emphasised in the literature is direct losses resulting from lending to institutions that turn out to be insolvent while the ELA is not sufficiently collateralised. The other cost is more indirect, resulting from moral hazard. ELA can affect the incentives of banks to make their own provisions against liquidity problems in the future; that is, instead of making adequate provisions themselves, banks may rely on expected ELA as insurance. Moreover, an expectation that ELA will effectively insure all bank creditors, and not just those covered by deposit insurance, can weaken market discipline.

Against the backdrop of these benefits and costs of lender of last resort actions, the literature focuses on three main questions: (i) how to distinguish between liquidity and solvency problems? (ii) how to contain moral hazard? and (iii) what is the actual responsibility of central banks as opposed to that of other agencies?

Illiquidity vs insolvency: who should receive ELA? In Bagehot's view, institutions without good collateral should not receive ELA, being assumed to be insolvent. However, when decisions on ELA need to be made quickly in practice, there may not be enough time to determine for sure whether a bank is solvent; and an originally solvent bank may become insolvent over the course of ELA provision.

Another view is that ELA should be provided not to individual banks but only to the market as a whole via open market operations, since liquidity would then be allocated to individual creditworthy banks via the interbank market (Goodfriend and King (1988), Bordo (1990), Schwartz (1992, 1995)). The effectiveness of this approach rests on the assumption that the central bank has no informational advantage over interbank market participants.

How to contain moral hazard? Views in the literature differ on how to address moral hazard. Bagehot (1873) argued that ELA should be provided at penalty rates and against good collateral, so that it is indeed a last resort and banks do not expect

---

[7]   As described in Carlson (2007), the Fed "eased short-term credit conditions by conducting more expansive open market operations at earlier-than-usual times, issuing public statements affirming its commitment to providing liquidity, and temporarily liberalizing the rules governing the lending of Treasury securities from its portfolio. [...] The Federal Reserve also encouraged the commercial banking system to extend liquidity support to other financial market participants."

to receive it "[...] as a matter of course", reducing moral hazard. Bagehot's rule of lending at a penalty rate was challenged later, and it was sometimes not applied to ELA (Goodhart and Schoenmaker (1995)); one reason given for this in the literature is that lending at a penalty rate could make the problems of a bank receiving ELA worse (Crockett (1996), Garcia and Plautz (1988)).

Another way to limit moral hazard is via "constructive ambiguity". Maintaining uncertainty about whether ELA will be provided can in principle incentivise banks to act prudently (Corrigan (1990), BIS (1997)). The same can be achieved by leaving open the conditions attached to possible ELA (Crockett (1996)). Constructive ambiguity leaves a large degree of discretion in the hands of decision-makers, giving rise to time-consistency problems.

What is the role of the central bank vs that of other agencies? The ability to supply reserves as riskless (domestic) assets in, in principle, unlimited amounts makes the central bank the natural lender of last resort. In addition, the central bank may have an informational advantage over the market because of its access to supervisory data. Many authors see the boundaries of central bank responsibilities as reached when ELA exposes the central bank to a potential loss. In this case, ELA would require a government guarantee to cover the central bank's exposure (Goodhart and Schoenmaker (1995)). Another view is that central banks do not need capital the same way as commercial banks (Stella (1997)) and can therefore shoulder some ELA-related credit risk.

2.2 Central banks' pre-crisis approaches

Domestic approaches. In practice, central banks (and public authorities responsible for financial crisis management) were reluctant to set out their approaches to ELA because of concerns about serious moral hazard and adverse effects on market functioning. By end-2006, about half of the central banks of the G10 advanced economies had publicly released statements on their ELA policies. Generally, these statements set out broad guidelines or principles for ELA. Many central banks, particularly in the euro area, were deliberately vague about their ELA policies, emphasising the importance of constructive ambiguity.

The growing recognition of the role of central banks in financial stability spurred the development of more explicit arrangements for crisis prevention and management in the years before 2007. Although for many constructive ambiguity remained a guiding principle, several central banks had started to speak more openly about their policies regarding ELA.

Such increased ex ante transparency was seen as a means for central banks to manage market expectations concerning the potential availability of ELA, thereby reducing the problem of moral hazard. For instance, public communication prior to the crisis indicated changes in delimiting the borders of possible ELA. In particular, the Swiss National Bank viewed only systemically important institutions as being eligible for ELA (implying that the range of eligible banks does not extend to all deposit-taking institutions). Other ex ante clarifications of central bank policies aimed at ensuring that technical preconditions for the provision of ELA were in place.

In all cases public communication remained consistent with a central bank's retention of full discretion as to how a policy would be implemented in practice. When ELA was provided, eligibility criteria and terms and conditions were generally guided by Bagehot's principles. Only solvent institutions were eligible for ELA, collateralisation was mandatory, and policy rates were the minimum price for ELA.

International approaches. The issue of cross-border ELA emerged in 1974 in the wake of the Herstatt collapse. In September 1974, G10 Governors issued a press communiqué on their lender of last resort function in euro-currency markets (BIS (1974)): "The Governors also had an exchange of views on the problem of the lender of last resort in the Euromarkets. They recognized that it would not be practical to lay down in advance detailed rules and procedures for the provision of temporary liquidity. But they were satisfied that to that end means are available and will be used if and when necessary."

The main instrument for providing ELA in foreign currency has been central bank swap lines. Previously, following 11 September 2001, the Federal Reserve had established temporary central bank swap lines for a duration of 30 days with the ECB and the Bank of England, and temporarily increased an existing swap line with the Bank of Canada. Their purpose was different from that of the swap network established during the financial crisis of 2008-09, in that they had been set up to provide emergency US dollar liquidity following disruptions in the financial infrastructure (see Moessner and Allen (2010b)).[8]

3. ELA during the crisis

During the financial crisis, central banks provided ELA of three sorts. First, they extended credit to prevent the disorderly failure of individual institutions perceived as systemically critical. Second, they stepped in for the malfunctioning interbank markets. And third, they provided funding to increase liquidity in specific financial markets.

3.1. Credit to individual troubled systemically critical institutions

The character of ELA provided to troubled institutions evolved with the crisis.[9] During a *first phase from September 2007 to August 2008* (before the Lehman default), ELA was provided to cover liquidity shortfalls due to an inability to obtain sufficient funding in interbank and other wholesale markets. Northern Rock, in September 2007, was unable to refinance securitised mortgages. In March 2008, Bear Stearns could not repay repurchase agreements (and other obligations) coming due the following day. The aim of ELA in these circumstances was to allow an orderly resolution of liquidity difficulties of financial institutions that were perceived as systemically important.

---

[8]   The cross-border provision of central bank liquidity in the form of currency swaps goes back to the 1920s and intensified in the 1960s (see Moessner and Allen (2010b) for an overview).

[9]   Annex 1 provides a more detailed description of the ELA provided to individual institutions from September 2007 to March 2009.

Already at this stage, ELA involved transactions with non-standard counterparties (see Table 1). In particular, the loan to Bear Stearns was the first time the Federal Reserve had used its authority to lend to non-banks since the 1930s. Moreover, the ELA entailed taking on what were likely to be greater than normal amounts of risk. While the collateral backing the loan extended to facilitate the acquisition of Bear Stearns by JPMorgan Chase consisted of investment-grade securities and performing loans and the loan was ultimately repaid in full, at times as the crisis worsened the value of the collateral fell below the amount of the loan from the Federal Reserve.[10]

In a **second stage of the crisis, following the collapse of Lehman Brothers**, central bank credit was provided in several cases – often in conjunction with government measures – to assist balance sheet restructuring. In September 2008, the Federal Reserve provided to American International Group (AIG) an $85 billion line of credit secured by all the assets of AIG and its primary non-regulated subsidiaries. The firm was unable to raise funds to post collateral to cover exposures related to declines in the prices of mortgage-related assets, and also faced an imminent downgrade in its credit rating. The Federal Reserve determined that the failure of AIG – a large insurance company and diversified financial services company with assets of over $1 trillion – only days after the failure of Lehman Brothers would have severely disrupted financial markets and "materially weakened economic performance".[11]

In October 2008, the Swiss National Bank (SNB) announced that it would finance the transfer of illiquid assets of UBS to a special purpose vehicle (SPV). UBS, one of the two largest Swiss banks, had announced record losses running into billions of Swiss francs at a time when the market's confidence in the big banks had been seriously eroded. Prices for credit default swaps (CDS) increased sharply, share prices plummeted, ratings were downgraded and the big banks' liquidity situation deteriorated (Swiss National Bank (2009)).

[10] See the appendix for additional information on the Bear Stearns transactions. In addition, the specific collateral requirements for the loan extended to facilitate the acquisition are described in http://www.newyorkfed.org/markets/maidenlane.html; the value of the collateral and the amount of the loan outstanding at a point where the collateral value was below the loan value is provided in "Federal Reserve System Monthly Report on Credit and Liquidity Programs and the Balance Sheet", June 2009, http://www.federalreserve.gov/monetarypolicy/files/monthlyclbsreport200906.pdf.

[11] "Report pursuant to Section 129 of the Emergency Economic Stabilization Act of 2008: Securities Borrowing Facility for the American International Group, Inc.", October 6, 2008, p 2.

Characteristics of central bank support provided to troubled institutions
between 2007 and 2009   Table 1

| Date | Institution | Problem | Central bank support measure | | | |
			Measure / objective	Instrument	Collateral	Pricing
14 Sep 2007	Northern Rock)	Inability to refinance securitised mortgages	Provision of liquidity facility to bridge funding gap	Callable loan	Mortgage-backed securities	
13 Mar 2008	Bear Stearns	Unable to repay repurchase agreements	Avoid disorderly default/facilitate merger with JPMorgan Chase	Collateralised loan/loan to SPV that acquired assets	Performing residential or commercial mortgages; investment grade securities	Primary credit rate
16 Sep 2008 (restructured several times)	AIG	Unable to meet collateral calls, imminent downgrade	Allow for orderly sale of assets	Revolving credit facility	All assets of AIG and primary non-regulated subsidiaries	Libor + 850 bp, reduced to Libor + 300 bp
16 Oct 2008	UBS	Large-scale writedowns on illiquid assets	Finance removal of assets from balance sheet	Long-term loan	Illiquid securitised assets	1-month Libor + 250 bp
23 Nov 2008	Citigroup	Potential losses hampering ability to obtain funding	Protection against declines in troubled assets	Non-recourse loan if losses sufficiently high (never used)	Mortgage-related assets	OIS + 300 bp
15 Jan 2009	Bank of America	Potential losses hampering ability to obtain funding	Protection against declines in troubled assets	Non-recourse loan if losses sufficiently high (never used)	Mortgage-related assets	OIS + 300 bp

In November 2008 the Federal Reserve joined the US Treasury and the Federal Deposit Insurance Corporation (FDIC) in providing Citigroup with protection against declines in value on a $306 billion pool of primarily mortgage-related assets.[12] In January 2009, the Federal Reserve, Treasury and FDIC provided similar protection for Bank of America on a $118 billion pool of loans, mortgage-related securities, corporate debt and derivatives. Further losses "... could have resulted in other financial institutions experiencing similar funding problems, posed risks to financial stability, and increased downside risks to economic growth".[13] Neither the Citigroup

[12]   "Report Pursuant to Section 129 of the Emergency Economic Stabilization Act of 2008: Authorization to Provide Residual Financing to Citigroup, Inc. for a Designated Asset Pool."

[13]   "Report Pursuant to Section 129 of the Emergency Economic Stabilization Act of 2008: Authorization to Provide Residual Financing to Bank of America Corporation Relating to a Designated Asset Pool", p. 3.

nor the Bank of America wraps were used, and the institutions paid exit fees to terminate the agreements.

In addition to providing credit to individual non-bank institutions under its emergency lending authority, the Federal Reserve System also provided ELA through the discount window to individual depository institutions that were experiencing financial difficulties. Institutions that are not financially sound do not qualify for the primary credit facility, but may be provided with secondary credit loans as a bridge to market sources of funds or to facilitate an orderly resolution. Secondary credit outstanding, which is usually zero, peaked at $985 million on 27 January 2010 (weekly average).

3.2. Credit extended to address a malfunctioning of interbank markets

Between August 2007 and early 2009, central banks expanded the provision of liquidity in response to three types of liquidity problems in the banking system as a whole (Table 2). First, insufficient access to reserves within the banking system was addressed by broadening the range of counterparties and eligible collateral, and easing the terms on standing lending facilities. Second, as the supply of term funding evaporated in interbank markets in autumn 2007, central banks conducted exceptional long-term open market operations. And third, shortages of foreign currency reserves were addressed by the establishment of central bank swap lines.

The extent to which central banks expanded their intermediation functions depended importantly on the ***design of pre-crisis operating frameworks***. These frameworks, designed and operated to implement a desired stance of monetary policy (Borio and Nelson (2008)), involved different degrees of intermediation by central banks. For instance, prior to the financial crisis, the Federal Reserve conducted monetary policy primarily by engaging in purchases and sales, either outright or through repurchase agreements (repos), of government securities, with a small group of broker-dealers referred to as "primary dealers". Primary dealers do not themselves have accounts at the Federal Reserve, so the initial impact of the open market operations is on the reserve balances of the banks where the primary dealers have accounts. Changes in reserve balances of primary dealers are distributed throughout the banking system using the interbank market and, in particular, the federal funds market.

In contrast, the ECB conducted its regular operations with a much broader range of counterparties and against a broad range of collateral. The main refinancing operations were repos with a weekly frequency and a maturity of normally one week, which are executed by the national central banks with a large number of counterparties against a range of marketable and non-marketable assets.

Measures taken to address liquidity problems in the banking system[1]							Table 2
	AU	**CA**	**EA**	**JP**	**CH**	**GB**	**US**
Insufficient access to reserves							
Broadening of counterparties						✓[3]	✓
Broadening of eligible collateral	✓	✓			✓[2]	✓	✓
Change in the standing lending facility						✓	✓
Shortage of term funding							
Exceptional long-term open market operations	✓	✓	✓	✓	✓	✓	✓
Shortage of reserves in foreign currency							
Central bank swap lines			✓	✓	✓	✓	✓

AU = Australia; CA = Canada; EA = euro area; JP = Japan; CH = Switzerland; GB = United Kingdom; US = United States. ✓ = yes; blank space = no.

[1] Table reflects information up to end-April 2008.   [2] Entered into effect on 1 October 2007, but not linked to the turmoil.   [3] Only for four special auctions of term funding announced in September 2007, for which, however, there were no bids.

Source: CGFS.

Addressing illiquidity in interbank markets. To facilitate an effective distribution of central bank funds, several central banks widened, either temporarily or permanently, the range of eligible collateral and counterparties. The Bank of England (BoE) offered four special three-month tenders in late September and October 2007 against a wider range of collateral and to a wider set of counterparties. As part of the coordinated central bank actions announced in December 2007, the BoE also widened the collateral list in, and increased the size of, its regular three-month repo operations.[14] The Bank of Canada (BoC) announced special operations in August 2007 that accepted temporarily as collateral all securities that were already eligible for its standing liquidity facility, and conducted some term repo operations in December and early 2008 that accepted a wider than normal range of collateral.[15] From September 2007, the Reserve Bank of Australia widened the list of collateral eligible for its regular repo operations and its overnight repo facility to include a broader range of bank paper, as well as residential mortgage-backed securities (RMBS) and asset-backed commercial paper (ABCP).

The Federal Reserve also eased, as one of the first responses to the crisis, the terms of access to the primary credit facility ("discount window"), its standing loan facility. Primary credit is intended to be used as a backup source of liquidity to address very short-term funding needs. Prior to the crisis, credit was typically extended on an overnight basis. The easing was intended to increase the liquidity of depository institutions and thereby support their ability to lend to businesses and households.

Stigma turned out to be a major impediment to the effectiveness of discount window lending in the United States (and, to some extent, that of the Bank of

---

[14] The widened collateral list includes AAA-rated RMBS and covered mortgage bonds.

[15] As part of its ongoing review of collateral policy, the BoC also decided to broaden the range of securities acceptable under the Standing Liquidity Facility to include certain types of ABCP (end-March 2008) and US Treasuries (expected by mid-2008).

England's Discount Window Facility). Even before the financial crisis, some banks were reluctant to borrow under the primary credit programme; they were willing to borrow in the interbank market at interest rates above the primary credit rate rather than turn to the window. During the crisis, banks' reluctance to use the window intensified. Even though the Federal Reserve had always kept information about individual borrowers confidential, banks were reportedly concerned that market participants might learn about their borrowing and view it as a sign of a weak financial condition.[16]

Provision of term funding. Following the evaporation of term funding in autumn 2007, all major central banks conducted exceptional long-term open market operations. As part of the December 2007 joint central bank announcement, the Federal Reserve established the Term Auction Facility (TAF). The TAF was intended to address heightened bank funding pressures and the issues of stigma associated with the primary credit programme. Under the TAF, the Federal Reserve auctioned credit to depository institutions. The TAF was established using the Federal Reserve's standard discount window authority, not its emergency authority.

The Eurosystem increased the provision of term funding through special longer-term refinancing operations. In August 2007, the ECB started to conduct supplementary three-month refinancing operations, and in March 2008 it announced two six-month refinancing operations (ECB (2008)). In June 2009, the ECB conducted a 12-month refinancing operation. The ECB in late 2008 moved to full allotments at fixed rate refinancing operations, thereby essentially establishing a fully elastic supply of central bank reserves. Other central banks, including the Swiss National Bank (SNB), the BoE and the Bank of Japan (BoJ), also expanded their provision of term funds.

Provision of liquidity in foreign currency. Banks' dependence on cross-border funding had grown rapidly prior to the crisis. Using BIS international banking statistics, McGuire and von Peter (2009) document the rapid expansion of foreign claims of reporting banks over the preceding decade. European banks, in particular, accumulated foreign claims at a pace that outstripped domestic credit growth. At the same time, banks also took on more foreign liabilities, reflecting a growing dependence on cross-border funding. UK, Swiss, German and Dutch banks built up large net foreign positions denominated in US dollars. Since these banks tended not to have a sufficiently large onshore dollar funding base while their US counterparts tended to have no structural needs for European currencies, cross-currency funding (borrowing in one currency to fund assets in another) was needed to fill the gap.[17]

The disruption to the interbank markets also impaired the ability of banking institutions outside the United States to secure necessary dollar funding. Early in the crisis, efforts by European banking institutions to secure funds in the US market early in the trading session led to large intraday swings in the federal funds rate.[18] Notwithstanding increasingly unfavourable borrowing conditions, the demand for cross-border funding, particularly in US dollars, remained high in part because institutions with longer-term US dollar investments were either unable to sell their

---

[16] As discussed below, the Dodd-Frank Act requires the Federal Reserve to publish information on individual borrowing going forward with a two-year lag.

[17] See CGFS (2010a) for a discussion of the need for foreign currency liquidity and the functioning of cross-border funding markets.

[18] "Central bank operations in response to the financial turmoil", *CGFS Papers*, no 31, July 2008, p 4.

assets because of illiquid markets or were unwilling to realise the losses that might ensue from doing so (CGFS (2010 (a)).

In order to facilitate the provision of dollars to foreign banking institutions, the Federal Reserve entered into dollar liquidity swap lines with a number of foreign central banks. The first lines were established in December 2007 with the ECB and the SNB. Swap lines were subsequently established with 12 other central banks.[19] Under the swap lines the foreign central bank would first purchase with its currency dollars from the Federal Reserve at prevailing market exchange rates; the dollars and foreign currencies were then swapped back at that same exchange rate at an agreed date in the future, as far ahead as three months. The foreign central bank paid the Federal Reserve interest, in many cases the interest it earned on its dollar loans or investments; the Federal Reserve maintained its foreign currency reserves at the foreign central bank and did not pay interest.

Shortages of foreign currency liquidity were largest in the US dollar, but also occurred in other currencies, and additional swap networks were set up between central banks during the 2007–09 crisis to relieve them, including a euro network under which the ECB supplied euros, a Swiss franc network and an Asian and Latin American network (see Allen and Moessner (2010)).

Use of the US dollar swap lines peaked in December 2008 at over $580 billion. In April 2009, the Federal Reserve established foreign currency liquidity swap lines with the BoE, ECB, BoJ and SNB that mirrored the dollar liquidity swap lines. The foreign currency swap lines, which were never used, would have allowed the Federal Reserve to acquire foreign currency to provide to US institutions. The dollar liquidity swap lines and foreign currency liquidity swap lines terminated on 1 February 2010. All loans were repaid in full (Graph 1). In May 2010, in response to the re-emergence of strains in short-term funding markets in Europe, the Federal Reserve reestablished dollar liquidity swap lines with the BoC, BoE, SNB, ECB and BoJ; on 31 October 2013, those lines were converted into standing arrangements that do not require periodic renewal.

- First, in late 2007 and especially in early 2008, haircuts on lower-quality collateral widened significantly and the range of collateral accepted in private repo transactions shrank (CGFS (2010b). The combination of a preference for secured funding and greater demand for liquid assets on the one hand and growing reluctance (or even unwillingness) to accept private assets, especially securitised products, on the other, resulted in a substantial collateral scarcity in key repo markets.

- Second, there were liquidity pressures on institutions outside the banking system. A significant part of the intermediation between borrowers and lenders in the United States occurs outside the banking system in what is sometimes referred to as the "shadow banking system".[20]

- Third, key markets for securities products became illiquid, curtailing the access of non-bank borrowers to credit. Uncertainty about their underlying value greatly reduced the demand for structured products, including asset- and mortgage backed securities, as well as covered bonds.

Alleviating collateral constraints in private funding markets. Several central banks responded by broadening the range of collateral accepted in central bank operations. This increased banks' scope for borrowing and, through collateral substitution, released higher-quality collateral for private market transactions. The Federal Reserve and the BoE introduced or increased securities lending programmes.

---

[20] The shadow banking system was estimated by Geithner (2008) to have been comparable in size in early 2007 to the traditional banking system: "In early 2007, asset-backed commercial paper conduits, in structured investment vehicles, in auction-rate preferred securities, tender option bonds and variable rate demand notes, had a combined asset size of roughly $2.2 trillion. Assets financed overnight in triparty repo grew to $2.5 trillion. Assets held in hedge funds grew to roughly $1.8 trillion. The combined balance sheets of the then five major investment banks totaled $4 trillion. In comparison, the total assets of the top five bank holding companies in the United States at that point were just over $6 trillion, and total assets of the entire banking system were about $10 trillion."

As noted above, the near failure of Bear Stearns and widespread counterparty credit concerns led to a severe disruption to the market for repurchase agreements, particularly those settled in the tri-party repo market.[21] At the peak in 2008, there was about $2.8 trillion in credit outstanding in the market, and it was a key source of finance for asset-backed securities (ABS) held by investment banks and securities lenders.[22] The impairment in the market "...degraded the ability of primary dealers to provide financing to participants in securitization markets."[23] As a result, in March 2008, the Federal Reserve used its emergency authority to lend to non-banks to establish two credit facilities for primary dealers: the **Term Securities Lending Facility** (TSLF) and the **Primary Dealer Credit Facility** (PDCF).

Under the **TSLF**, established on 11 March 2008,[24] the Federal Reserve auctioned loans of US Treasury securities to primary dealers. In exchange it accepted other Treasury securities, agency debt, agency mortgage-backed securities (MBS) and non-agency triple-A rated private label MBS. On 14 September 2008, eligible collateral was extended to include all investment grade debt securities.[25] At its peak in October 2008, the Federal Reserve lent out over $230 billion in Treasury securities under the TSLF. The TSLF was closed on 1 February 2010. All securities loans were repaid in full.

The **PDCF** was established on 16 March 2008 to provide further liquidity support to the tri-party repo market and the primary dealers. Under the PDCF, the Federal Reserve extended overnight loans to primary dealers. Initially, the eligible collateral was Treasury, agency and private investment grade debt securities, but on 15 September 2008, in the wake of the Lehman failure, the collateral was extended to include all securities eligible for pledging in the tri-party repo market, which includes some whole loans as well as below-investment-grade or even unrated securities. The credit extended under the PDCF peaked at around $150 billion at the end of September 2009. The PDCF was closed on 1 February 2010. All loans were repaid in full.

In April 2008, the BoE introduced the **Special Liquidity Scheme**, a facility in which banks could swap temporarily illiquid assets for UK Treasury bills. The asset swaps had terms of one year (renewable to up to three years).

The ECB did not provide a collateral swap arrangement, but **broadened its collateral framework**, accepting a substitution of liquid collateral pledged in ECB operations with temporary illiquid assets, especially ABS. The eligibility of ABS originated by the pledging bank as collateral in Eurosystem refinancing operations supported ABS issuance in the euro area. The annual average share of ABS pledged

---

[21] In the tri-party repo market, borrowers receive short-term, usually overnight, financing for securities by selling them with an agreement to repurchase them. The collateral in the tri-party market is held at a third party.

[22] "Tri-Party Repo Infrastructure Reform Task Force Report", p 3. Appendix II to "Tri-Party Repo Infrastructure Reform, A White Paper Prepared by The Federal Reserve Bank of New York", 17 May 2010.

[23] "Report Pursuant to Section 129 of the Emergency Economic Stabilization Act of 2008: Primary Dealer Credit Facility and Other Credit for Broker-Dealers."

[24] "Report Pursuant to Section 129 of the Emergency Economic Stabilization Act of 2008: Term Securities Lending Facility."

[25] Press release, Board of Governors of the Federal Reserve System, 14 September 2008.

with the Eurosystem rose from 6% in 2004 to 28% during 2008 (Cheun, Köppen-Mertes and Weller (2009)).

Liquidity provision to "shadow banks". On 16 September 2008, a prominent money market mutual fund (MMMF) announced that it had "broken the buck", that is, it would repay investments at less than dollar-for-dollar, as a result of losses on its holdings of Lehman debt. Over the following four weeks, investors withdrew about $450 billion in deposits from prime money funds – money funds that invest in high quality private money market instruments as well as government securities – whose assets equalled $2.2 trillion just prior to the outflows. Prime funds responded by reducing their investments in money market instruments, including commercial paper, and shortening the maturity on the instruments they did buy.

In order to help money market investors meet redemptions and improve liquidity in money markets, the Federal Reserve established three credit facilities: the ***Asset-Backed Commercial Paper Money Market Mutual Fund Liquidity Facility*** (AMLF), the ***Commercial Paper Funding Facility*** (CPFF) and the ***Money Market Investor Funding Facility*** (MMIFF). A fourth facility, the ***Direct Money Market Mutual Fund Lending Facility*** (DMLF) was authorised but not implemented after the Federal Reserve received reports that money funds would be unwilling to use it.[26]

The ***AMLF*** was authorised by the Federal Reserve on 19 September 2008.[27] Under the AMLF, the Federal Reserve extended credit to depository institutions, bank holding companies, and branches and agencies of foreign banks to finance their purchases of top-rated asset-backed commercial paper (ABCP) from MMMFs. The facility was intended to help MMMFs holding ABCP finance redemptions by investors. The Federal Reserve provided the funds on a non-recourse basis (that is, the borrower could surrender the collateral in lieu of repayment) and lent the full amortised cost of the ABCP (that is, there was no haircut). Consequently, the Federal Reserve took all the credit risk on the ABCP. The amount lent under the AMLF peaked at over $150 billion at the beginning of October 2008. The AMLF closed on 1 February 2010. All loans were repaid in full.

On 7 October 2008, the Federal Reserve established the ***CPFF***. Under the CPFF, the Federal Reserve lent to a special purpose vehicle (SPV) that in turn purchased top-rated three-month commercial paper directly from eligible issuers. By eliminating the risk that eligible issuers would be unable to roll over their CP, the CPFF was intended to encourage investors to be willing to hold longer-term CP. The SPV purchased ABCP discounted at a rate equal to 300 basis points plus the overnight index swap (OIS) rate, and 100 basis points plus the OIS rate for unsecured CP.[28] Unsecured CP issuers also paid a 100 basis point fee. The CP holdings of the CPFF SPV peaked at about $350 billion in January 2009. The facility was closed on 1 February 2009. All commercial paper and loans to the SPV were repaid in full.

---

[26]   See Minutes of Meeting of Federal Reserve Board, "Financial Markets – Proposal to Provide Liquidity Directly to Money Market Mutual Funds through the Direct Money Market Mutual Fund Lending Facility (103 KB PDF)", 3 October 2008, pp 11–12, and "Bagehot's Dictum in Practice: Formulating and Implementing Policies to Combat the Financial Crisis", speech by Brian Madigan on 21 August 2009, p 7. http://www.federalreserve.gov/newsevents/speech/madigan20090821a.htm

[27]   "Report Pursuant to Section 129 of the Emergency Economic Stabilization Act of 2008: Asset-Backed Commercial Paper Money Market Mutual Fund Liquidity Facility."

[28]   OIS rates equal approximately the expected federal funds rate.

In addition, on 21 October 2008, the Federal Reserve established the **MMIFF**.[29] Under the MMIFF, the Federal Reserve would have lent to a series of SPVs to finance 90% of their purchases of certain high-quality certificates of deposit, banknotes and CP from eligible money market investors – money market mutual funds or similar. For each dollar of assets purchased, the SPVs would have provided the money funds 90 cents plus a 10 cent claim on the assets of the SPV that was junior to the Federal Reserve's claim. The MMIFF was intended to be a source of liquidity for money funds. The MMIFF was never used, probably because there was no renewal of the severe outflows from money funds. It was closed on 30 October 2009.

Reducing illiquidity premia in credit markets. In the wake of the turmoil caused by the Lehman default and the turmoil in money markets, new issuance of ABS declined sharply in the third quarter of 2008 and virtually ceased in October 2008. The ABS markets historically have funded a substantial share of consumer and small-business loans. Similarly, the commercial mortgage-backed securities (CMBS) market, which had financed approximately 20% of outstanding commercial mortgages, came to a standstill in mid-2008. Continued disruption of these markets could have significantly limited the availability of credit to households and businesses, further weakening US economic activity.

On 25 November 2008, the Federal Reserve and Treasury announced the creation of the **Term Asset-Backed Securities Loan Facility (TALF)** to promote renewed issuance of ABS, thereby increasing the availability of credit to households and small businesses.[30] The subsequent inclusion of CMBS as eligible collateral for TALF was intended to help borrowers finance new purchases of commercial properties or refinance existing commercial mortgages on better terms. Under the TALF, the Federal Reserve extended non-recourse loans to investors in certain AAA-rated ABS. The TALF initially accepted newly issued ABS backed by consumer loans and small business loans.

Over time, it was expanded to include certain other classes of ABS backed by business loans and newly issued and legacy CMBS. The TALF loans were collateralised by the securities purchased and were extended in amounts that were less than the value of the securities by haircuts that varied depending on the risk of the collateral. The loans were extended with maturities of three years or five years, on a non-recourse basis, and at interest rates chosen to be above those in more normal conditions. Specifically, the interest rates were mostly set at Libor plus 100 basis points or an equivalent fixed rate, although the spread was reduced to 50 basis points when the collateral benefited from a government guarantee.

The US Treasury Department – under the Troubled Assets Relief Program (TARP) of the Emergency Economic Stabilization Act of 2008 – provided $20 billion of credit protection to the Federal Reserve in connection with the TALF. The TALF closed on 30 June 2009. When it closed, there was about $43 billion in TALF loans outstanding. On 19 February 2014, there was $96 million outstanding and all the securities backing the loans were AAA-rated.

---

[29] "Report Pursuant to Section 129 of the Emergency Economic Stabilization Act of 2008: Money Market Investor Funding Facility."

[30] "Report Pursuant to Section 129 of the Emergency Economic Stabilization Act of 2008: Term Asset-Backed Securities Loan Facility."

On 6 July 2009 the Eurosystem initiated the covered bond purchase programme (CBPP), under which it intended to purchase eligible covered bonds, with a targeted nominal amount of €60 billion. Liquidity in the covered bond market, which is an important source of funding for European banks, had deteriorated substantially against the backdrop of mounting investor concerns about collateral quality. The covered bond purchase programme was completed by end-June 2010 (Graph 2).

Photo Removed Due to Copyright Restrictions

3.4. Observations and issues raised by ELA during the crisis

During the crisis, the provision of ELA evolved with changing perceptions of the sources and character of systemic risk. Yet in many ways central banks still exercised their lender of last resort function in a manner consistent with the pre-crisis views of the **objectives** of ELA, namely to avoid the costly failure of individual institutions and to limit the risk of contagion (Madigan (2009)). For example, by providing liquidity to help MMMFs meet withdrawals, the Federal Reserve prevented a fire sale of assets that would have driven down asset values further, leading to more money funds "breaking the buck" and yet more investor withdrawals. By providing abundant liquidity, the Federal Reserve was preventing a classic bank run.

Central banks also generally adhered to broad pre-crisis lender of last resort **principles** when providing ELA to individual financial institutions. In most cases, loans were backed by good collateral, were short-term, and were at rates that were a penalty to those that prevailed in normal times although below those that prevailed at the height of the crisis. All loans provided by the Federal Reserve were repaid in full or are expected to be repaid in full. Moreover, the use of many ELA facilities –

including the Federal Reserve's lending facilities and the dollar swaps provided by a number of central banks – declined rapidly as the financial situation normalised.

However, as the turmoil evolved into a systemic liquidity crisis it became increasingly challenging to adhere to Bagehot's criteria. The value of financial assets became increasingly dependent on the perceived ability of financial institutions to fund positions. In turn, the funding market access of financial market institutions was impaired by uncertainty about asset values and their solvency.

Distinguishing illiquidity from insolvency. In the course of the crisis it became more difficult, if not impossible, to distinguish between institutions that were illiquid but solvent, and insolvent ones. In part, this reflected the fact that solvency depended on the illiquidity discount of institutions' assets. In particular, an institution's assets might be worth less than its liabilities at fire-sale prices, but it could be viable as a going concern if a liquidity default could be avoided. For example, although AIG had insufficient liquid assets to meet its immediate obligations, the credit extended by the US government and the Federal Reserve (which was backed by substantial but illiquid collateral) allowed the firm to liquidate some of its assets over time, meet its obligations, repay the government loan and return to viability. Similarly, transferring illiquid UBS assets into the Swiss National Bank's SPV prevented fire sales of these assets.

Lending against good collateral. Central banks in some cases lent to systemically critical institutions against sufficient but illiquid and risky assets. In these cases, the benefit of the central bank actions depended, in large part, on limiting the concerns of market participants about the ability of the troubled institution to obtain funding or about the exposure of the institution to future losses on riskier assets. For example, the Bank of England lent HBOS and Royal Bank of Scotland UK Treasury bills against unsecuritised mortgage and loan assets.

In several instances, including the protection provided to Citi and Bank of America, the extension of credit to AIG and the TALF, the Treasury absorbed the lion's share of the credit risk with the Federal Reserve either latently or actually providing most of the funding. This arrangement appropriately put the risk with the fiscal authority and left the Federal Reserve with the virtually riskless obligations that are consistent with traditional central banking principles. Although these arrangements required cooperation between the Federal Reserve, Treasury and other agencies, a joint Department of Treasury – Federal Reserve press release on 23 March 2009 emphasised that the Federal Reserve had sole responsibility for maintaining monetary stability and set monetary policy independently.[31]

Finally, there are questions as to whether, in some cases, direct purchases of illiquid, high-quality securities would have been more effective than collateralised lending to financial institutions.[32] For instance, when designing the AMLF, the Federal Reserve extended non-recourse loans to banks without a haircut to finance purchases of ABCP. From the perspective of risk, the transactions were virtually the same as if the Federal Reserve had bought the paper, except that the yield on the ABCP above

[31]   "The Role of the Federal Reserve in Preserving Financial and Monetary Stability. Joint Statement by the Department of the Treasury and the Federal Reserve", 23 March 2009, http://www.federalreserve.gov/newsevents/press/monetary/20090323b.htm.

[32]   The Federal Reserve does not have the authority to purchase private securities.

the primary credit rate was earned by the commercial banks to give them an incentive to participate.

Lending at penalty rates. Lending at a penalty rate may have reduced the effectiveness of ELA in the early stage of the crisis at least in some cases. When providing additional liquidity as a backup, charging above market rates added to stigma at the Federal Reserve's discount window and, as noted above, possibly the Bank of England's Discount Window Facility (see Fisher (2012) for a discussion). Hence, stigma significantly reduced the effectiveness of a principal tool for providing ELA. A discount window-type facility is not beneficial for relieving pressures in financial markets if institutions will go to extraordinary lengths to avoid using it.

Moreover, penalty rates may have been counterproductive when the central bank was providing a source of funding rather than a backup source of liquidity. For example, by providing credit at a market rate to commercial banks through the Term Auction Facility, the Federal Reserve sought to replace term funding that had evaporated, supporting the ability of the banks to provide credit to businesses and households. The ECB introduced a fixed rate full allotment tender procedure from October 2008, which provided eligible euro area financial institutions with unlimited access to central bank liquidity at the ECB's main refinancing rate, subject to adequate collateral (Cour-Thimann and Winkler (2013)).

Constructive ambiguity. At a certain point in the financial crisis, when the system became too fragile to withstand the disruption associated with a major failure, constructive ambiguity was seen as becoming impossible. That was true not only for banks, but also for bank-like institutions. In those circumstances, the list of institutions that were seen as too important to be allowed to fail expanded dramatically. It would probably not have been credible to attempt to limit moral hazard by indicating that there was a possibility that the central bank would withhold ELA that it was legally able to provide and allow a disruptive failure. Against this backdrop, it is questionable whether constructive ambiguity is a viable policy option in the future.

ELA in foreign currency. Lastly, given the international nature of financial institutions and markets, institutions can need ELA in foreign currencies, especially when foreign exchange markets are disrupted. The foreign currency swap lines were an efficient mechanism to provide central banks with the means to extend foreign currency ELA. A particular advantage of the arrangements was that the foreign central bank incurred any credit risk associated with lending to the foreign banking organisation and also made the lending decision.

4. A post-crisis view of ELA

The unprecedented scale and scope of the ELA provided in 2007–09 helped to prevent a collapse of the global financial system. But, as discussed in the previous section, it was not without costs and it presented a number of challenges. First, even though central banks have incurred only limited direct losses from ELA, the ELA lending was in many instances riskier than normal lending. Second, by taking on risk and by widening the range of institutions that received ELA beyond central banks' traditional counterparties, the lending risked increasing moral hazard. In light of the scale and scope of ELA, market participants, particularly those that were not previously seen as covered by the lender-of-last-resort safety net, may now see the odds of benefiting from ELA in the future as higher than before the crisis. Third, in some cases, central banks needed to develop new arrangements to address liquidity needs outside the banking sector in great haste, risking mistakes in execution and posing material communication challenges. Fourth, because the ELA required the central bank to provide liquidity in new ways, it also obliged it to make difficult choices about where to draw boundaries. Fifth, the provision of ELA in many cases required that the central bank design and execute programmes jointly with the fiscal authority, and develop risk-sharing arrangements with the fiscal authority, arrangements that require careful consideration to ensure continued central bank independence with respect to monetary policy. And sixth, because the frequency and nature of ELA strengthened the view among investors, bank managements and supervisors that borrowing from the central bank was an indication that a financial institution was in trouble, and because of the unpopularity of ELA, the stigma associated with central bank lending worsened significantly.

The costs and challenges, as well as the important role of central banks in responding to the financial crisis, shaped the post-crisis view of financial institution liquidity, central bank lending in general, and ELA in particular.[33] Financial institutions, as well as the supervisors and regulators of financial institutions, have raised their assessments of the amount and quality of capital and liquidity necessary to keep the odds that ELA will be needed in the future acceptably low. Relatedly, the anticipated role of central banks in responding to a financial crisis has changed, with a reduced expectation that they would lend to individual institutions to address idiosyncratic problems, but perhaps an increased expectation that they would address systemic liquidity pressures throughout the financial system. The latter consideration extends to the need to provide liquidity in foreign currencies and also to the need to reduce stigma.

4.1. Self-insurance, regulation and moral hazard

The costs and risks incurred providing ELA during the crisis suggest that the financial system needs to be more resilient if the likelihood of needing ELA in the future is to be significantly reduced. International banks' capital buffers were too slim and of insufficient quality to absorb losses, let alone to reassure market participants of banks' soundness. Several factors arguably contributed to insufficient self-insurance before the crisis, including weaknesses in the assessment and management of liquidity risk by financial institutions; a regulatory framework that did not place sufficient emphasis on the adequacy of capital and liquidity buffers; and a lack of market discipline. The consensus that increased and higher-quality liquidity and capital levels are necessary at financial institutions has been reflected both in the behaviour of the private sector and in the new post-crisis regulatory architecture.

Assessment and management of liquidity risk. The financial crisis has shifted the focus of bank risk management and regulatory authorities to liquidity risk. This shift is evident in the increasing number of papers and guidelines on this topic, and the room devoted to liquidity in financial reports. The increased focus on liquidity risk is also visible in the change in the funding approaches of international banks, which aim at reducing liquidity mismatches and the reliance on unstable wholesale funding

---

[33]   Carlson et al (2014) provide additional discussion of how the Federal Reserve's lending during the crisis illustrates why liquidity regulations are necessary despite the existence of a lender of last resort.

(BIS (2014)), and the accumulation of liquid assets well ahead of the introduction of the new liquidity standards

It is, however, an open question to what extent enhancements in liquidity risk measurement and management can take into account the endogenous nature of liquidity. Market and funding liquidity are dependent on the willingness of market participants to trade and provide funding. Hence, liquidity conditions are inherently fragile. Even conservative liquidity risk management may not fully capture this risk. For instance, the range of securities that can reliably be traded, and posted as collateral, in a systemic crisis may turn out to be much smaller than expected. Moreover, when an institution experiences a liquidity shortfall and pulls back from lending to other institutions, sells assets at fire-sale prices, or even defaults, it imposes costs on other institutions that it does not necessarily internalise. As a consequence, even though the financial crisis experiences have given each financial institution incentives to strengthen its capital and liquidity positions, there are good reasons to suspect that those individual efforts will fall short of the social optimum, pointing to the importance of a tightening of regulations.

Financial regulation. The substantial regulatory reforms that have been put in place since the crisis are likely to have reduced the odds of future crises and associated large-scale ELA. The Basel III capital and liquidity rules require banks to hold more and higher-quality capital (see BCBS (2010), and BCBS (2014) on implementation progress). Moreover, Basel III for the first time establishes a global minimum standard for bank liquidity. The Liquidity Coverage Ratio (LCR) defines minimum requirements in terms of liquid asset holdings, while the Net Stable Funding Ratio (NSFR) aims at containing maturity mismatches on bank balance sheets. More stringent capital standards should reduce the likelihood of bank funding strains because of counterparty risk concerns.

For regulatory measures to effectively reduce the need for ELA, at least two conditions need to be met. First, ***liquidity regulation*** needs to be designed in a way that encourages prudent liquidity management in tranquil periods and allows the use of liquidity buffers to cushion a liquidity shock. For example, the LCR aims to provide banks with the ability to sustain operations for 30 days by drawing down their buffer stocks of liquid assets rather than resorting to government assistance. In addition, requiring institutions to maintain strong liquidity buffers may also facilitate a wind-down without a need to draw on ELA.

Yet a systemic liquidity shock may require an infusion of liquidity into the financial system. For instance, banks may hoard liquid assets over and above those necessary to satisfy the regulatory requirement for precautionary reasons. And banks may be reluctant to use liquidity buffers and let the LCR drop because of fears of stigma (Stein (2013)). As a consequence, more stringent liquidity regulation can be expected to reduce the need for ELA in response to idiosyncratic events and to make systemic events less likely. But it is not clear to what extent such regulation would, or should be intended to, reduce the need for liquidity injections by central banks if a systemic liquidity crisis were to occur.

Second, the ***perimeter of regulation*** would have to cover institutions that can be the source of liquidity shocks with system-wide effects. For example, as discussed above and also concluded by Pozsar et al (2010), the Federal Reserve provided a backstop to credit intermediation by the largely unregulated shadow banking system, as well as to traditional banks for their exposure to the shadow banking system, by acting as lender of last resort through its liquidity facilities. The resulting increase in moral hazard may have been considerable because the ELA appeared to extend the safety net to a large new set of largely unregulated institutions.

Fundamental economic forces may contribute to the risk that ELA will be necessary for institutions outside the regulated sector. Households and businesses have a large and inelastic demand for maturity transformation – eg, for demand deposits and long-term loans. Higher capital and liquidity buffers and limits on maturity mismatches make maturity transformation within the banking system more expensive and create incentives to provide it outside the regulated sector. As a result, financial regulators will need to continuously monitor developments in the financial system to identify where maturity transformation is taking place, consider the implications for liquidity risks in the financial system, and consider policy measures to contain moral hazard.

Moral hazard. The extent to which lender of last resort actions during the crisis have resulted in an increase in moral hazard that has not been checked by subsequent regulatory changes remains an open question. There are arguments on both sides. On the one hand, there is progress in policy initiatives that aim at internalising the effects of excessive risk-taking. Perhaps most importantly, there has been some progress in establishing bank resolution frameworks (Tucker (2014)). Effective bank resolution frameworks would strengthen market discipline and reduce incentives of bank management for risk taking.

On the other hand, it may be challenging to contain moral hazard in certain parts of the financial system. As mentioned before, non-bank entities that benefited from ELA may expect similar support in case of another crisis. Systemically important banks raise another set of issues. As pointed out by Tucker (2009), measures to contain risk-taking by such institutions, for instance a restrictive central bank collateral policy, may face a time consistency problem. This is because of the expectation that the central bank will have to relax these policies in case of a liquidity shock in view of contagion risk. This underlines the need to address the "too big to fail" problem in an effective and credible manner.

4.2. Mechanisms for providing ELA in the future

The review of central bank actions during the financial crisis points to some common principles that appear likely to characterise the design of the mechanisms through which ELA would be provided in the future if needed.

- First, greater resilience of the financial system as well as new mechanisms to resolve a troubled institution at lower cost appear likely to lead to a reduced role for the central bank in providing ELA to individual institutions on a discretionary basis.

- Second, changes in the role of non-bank, possibly unregulated, institutions and markets in providing liquidity may require considerable flexibility in dealing with system-wide liquidity strains. One aspect is to ensure that operating frameworks can deal effectively with interbank market stress. Another aspect concerns the potential need to support a broader range of institutions and markets, including the provision of credit in foreign currencies. Reducing the stigma associated with borrowing from the central bank is necessary for central bank lending to be an effective tool for addressing systemic strains.

The role of the central bank. On balance, post-crisis developments seem likely to reduce the role of the central bank in providing ELA to individual institutions. Stronger liquidity buffers should give authorities more time to assess the systemic implications of denying support and decide on ELA measures (Santos and Suarez (2014)). And the existence of workable bank resolution regimes would clarify the role of ELA when unwinding an institution that turns out to be insolvent. Indeed, in the United States the FDIC now has the authority to resolve a failing systemically important institution in an orderly way and, with the approval of the Secretary of the Treasury, provide it with ELA if necessary.

However, the situation may be different in case of a systemic liquidity shock. In this case, the traditional arguments for the central bank acting as lender of last resort may be particularly important – it can create virtually unlimited funds instantaneously, while liquidity failures at systemically critical institutions can materialise in days or even hours.[34] This, in turn, may require closer cooperation between supervisory authorities and the central bank, especially for systemically important institutions, collective oversight arrangements or a reallocation of supervisory powers. In the United States, for instance, all non-bank financial companies that are determined by the new Financial Stability Oversight Council to be systemically significant are subject to consolidated supervision by the Federal Reserve.

Systemic liquidity stress. Central banks should be equipped to deal with a systemic liquidity crisis that requires the provision of ELA to markets. In terms of operational capabilities the crisis has demonstrated that operational frameworks can be adjusted quickly when needed. However, it might be useful for central banks to retain, and strengthen, measures that can mitigate immediate stress in interbank markets arising from a systemic liquidity shock (Domanski (2010)). These include (i) ***standing lending facilities that are free of stigma***, (ii) ***regular provision of term funding***, and (iii) ***a wider range of collateral in certain operations*** that are likely to be of particular importance in stress situations, eg term funding operations.[35]

ELA may also be needed to replace other malfunctioning markets. The provision of ELA to markets required central banks to expand their counterparties and the collateral they accept. All interventions entail boundaries, and it is critical that the boundaries are determined by principles, minimising credit allocation. For instance, since there are hundreds of different kinds of ABS, the TALF accepted the major categories but not some smaller types of ABS. Similarly, the TALF accepted legacy and new-issue CMBS, but not legacy or new-issue RMBS. The choice was governed by an

---

[34] Legislation in the United States has moved in the direction of restricting the Federal Reserve's power to provide ELA to individual financial institutions in future. The recent amendment to Federal Reserve Act 13.3, enacted in 2010, prohibits the Fed from providing ELA to individual institutions. The 2010 amendment stipulates that "Such policies and procedures shall be designed to ensure that any emergency lending program or facility is for the purpose of providing liquidity to the financial system, and not to aid a failing financial company, and that the security for emergency loans is sufficient to protect taxpayers from losses and that any such program is terminated in a timely and orderly fashion." This amendment will prevent the Fed from acting as lender of last resort to individual non-depository institutions in a future crisis. It also requires the Fed to have prior approval of the Secretary of the Treasury for ELA under Federal Reserve Act 13(3).

[35] See Tucker (2009).

objective of providing support for the market for ABS broadly, but also by what could safely and expediently be taken as collateral.[36]

There also does not appear to be any reason apart from legal restrictions why the extension of credit should only be in the form of a loan. Purchasing a low-risk short-term security, as is done by many central banks, would appear to be an equivalent and at times superior approach. These arrangements continue to be well-suited for lender of last resort credit provided by a central bank as a backup source of credit to sound institutions. Since such credit is typically provided either to support monetary policy operations or to meet late-in-the-day transitory funding needs, it can only be provided by the central bank because only central bank lending creates reserve balances and, as the operator of the payment system, the central bank is the payment platform that is last to close.

ELA need not be limited to loans extended with recourse to the borrower. One advantage of recourse lending is that repayment comes first from the financial resources of the borrower. If the recourse loan is collateralised, the collateral offers a secondary source of repayment. However, ELA may require lending to new counterparties whose financial condition cannot be readily assessed or in situations where it might be counterproductive for the central bank to expose the borrowers to the risk that the collateral would decline in value. Providing non-recourse loans in such circumstances may be economically nearly the same as purchasing the underlying collateral, and such purchases may at times be the superior option.

ELA in foreign currencies. As with the need for ELA in domestic currency, the best option would be to prevent international liquidity problems from occurring in the first place. This could be achieved in various ways, including (i) via capital and liquidity regulation, which is being tightened following the crisis, and which is likely to lead to reduced currency or maturity mismatches; and (ii) further strengthening foreign exchange market infrastructure (see CGFS (2010a) for a detailed discussion).[37] However, prevention may not be fully effective, so it is also important to consider how international liquidity could be provided in a future crisis (see Moessner and Allen (2010a)).

The extension of US dollar central bank swap lines across a wider number of time zones in the aftermath of the Lehman bankruptcy was arguably a potent and appropriate remedy for the acute, global-scale US dollar shortage at the time. In some jurisdictions, merely the announcement of having established a swap arrangement with the Federal Reserve as backstop was apparently sufficient to bolster confidence among market participants, making it unnecessary to draw on the swap line (eg in Brazil and Singapore).[38]

Central bank swap or repo lines are one obvious candidate solution for systemic liquidity problems such as the global US dollar liquidity shortage observed in the

---

[36] Joint Press Release, Board of Governors of the Federal Reserve System and Department of Treasury, 3 March 2009.

[37] See for example the new liquidity standards by the Basel Committee on Banking Supervision, self-sufficiency rules for liquidity purposes in the new liquidity regime of the UK Financial Services Authority, and proposed limits to banks' exposures in the European Commission's capital requirement directive (BCBS (2009, 2010), FSA (2009), European Commission (2008)).

[38] In some other countries (eg Canada), the swap lines were not drawn because US dollar liquidity shortages and the FX swap market disruptions were not as serious as elsewhere.

recent crisis. For less systemic problems, however, it is less obvious that such arrangements would be part of the solution. There are different views as to how desirable it is for central banks to establish, ex ante, scenarios that might warrant such arrangements. While there may be value in having guiding principles for the use of such facilities that are generally understood among central banks, it is also important that inter-central bank arrangements should be kept flexible, allowing sufficient room to use discretion to respond to different situations. Recent experience shows that when circumstances warrant, the swap arrangements can be put in place quickly and on a scale commensurate with the circumstances.

Stigma. Central bank lending can only be a useful tool for addressing systemic liquidity strains if financial institutions are willing to borrow from the central bank. Stigma is a serious impediment to such borrowing, and it is extremely difficult to reduce. During a financial crisis, almost by definition there are widespread doubts about counterparty liquidity and creditworthiness. As long as tapping central bank credit is seen as potentially signalling weakness, stigma will persist and will probably be severe in a crisis. The perception that borrowing will signal weakness does not need to be based on reality to cause stigma. If bank managements, investors and supervisors see the use of central bank liquidity as a signal that something is wrong, banks will avoid borrowing at the central bank. Indeed, given the use of central bank liquidity to fund weak institutions during the financial crisis, stigma may probably be worse going forward in the absence of additional steps to reduce it. Moreover, in the United States, the Federal Reserve is now required to disclose, albeit with a considerable lag, the identities of borrowers.[39]

There are different ways that stigma can potentially be reduced. Borrowing from central banks can be made more regular and familiar to institutions – the Eurosystem largely avoided stigma during the crisis in part because borrowing is seen as unremarkable. The association between borrowing and historical instances of liquidity support can be weakened. And borrowing can be made less likely to be seen as an indication of weakness, for instance by lending against a narrower set of collateral.[40]

---

[39] Loans to depository institutions will be disclosed after a two-year lag; loans to non-depository institutions extended through credit facilities established the Federal Reserve's 13(3) emergency lending authority will be disclosed one year after the credit facility is closed.

[40] See Tucker (2009) for a discussion of possible approaches towards dealing with stigma.

Annex 1: liquidity support to individual institutions, 2007–09

September 2007 – August 2008

On Friday 14 September 2007, the Bank of England established a liquidity support facility for **Northern Rock** that provided collateralised loans at a penalty interest rate. The decision to provide a liquidity support facility to Northern Rock reflected the difficulties the institution had accessing longer-term funding and the mortgage securitisation market, on which it was particularly reliant.[41] The Treasury Committee characterised Northern Rock's problems as follows: "The high-risk, reckless business strategy of Northern Rock, with its reliance on short- and medium-term wholesale funding and an absence of sufficient insurance and a failure to arrange standby facility or cover that risk, meant that it was unable to cope with the liquidity pressures placed upon it by the freezing of international capital markets in August 2007" (House of Commons Treasury Committee (2008)).

The Governor of the Bank of England characterised Northern Rock's problems as follows: "It was the business strategy that was fatally flawed in this episode where, once those markets had closed in mortgage backed securities, they were absolutely unable to finance their wholly illiquid assets" (House of Commons Treasury Committee (2008)). He noted Northern Rock's insufficient liquidity insurance, and concluded that: "So when it came to the Bank of England for support, it was important that liquidity was not provided free" (House of Commons Treasury Committee (2008), King (2007)). The announcement of the liquidity facility stated that "This liquidity facility will be available to help Northern Rock to fund its operations during the current period of turbulence in financial markets while Northern Rock works to secure an orderly resolution to its current liquidity problems ... The FSA judges that Northern Rock is solvent, exceeds its regulatory capital requirement and has a good quality loan book" (Bank of England (2007a)). The Tripartite authorities, comprising the Bank of England, HM Treasury and the Financial Services Authority, viewed Northern Rock as posing a systemic risk (House of Commons Treasury Committee (2008)).

On October 9 2007, the Bank of England announced that it would make available additional liquidity support to Northern Rock (Bank of England (2007b)), and further information was given by the Treasury, which provided an indemnity to the Bank of England, on 11 October (HM Treasury (2007)). This support, without a specific borrowing limit and secured against all assets of Northern Rock, was provided to enable the firm to pursue a full range of restructuring options. The Northern Rock case was the first time for many years that the Bank of England had undertaken a lender of last resort operation for a major bank.

On Thursday March 13 2008, **Bear Stearns** informed the Federal Reserve that it was going to be unable to repay its repurchase agreements and other obligations coming due on the following day. At that time, Bear Stearns was one of the largest securities firms in the United States, and its default would have severely disrupted financial markets, particularly the critical market for repurchase agreements. On Friday March 14 2008, the Federal Reserve lent $12.9 billion to Bear Stearns against

---

[41] See "The run on the Rock", House of Commons Treasury Committee, 24 January 2008.

$13.8 billion in collateral.[42] The loan was extended at the then prevailing primary credit rate (the rate at which the Federal Reserve lends to financially sound banks, often called the discount rate) of 2.25%. The loan was provided to avoid a default by Bear Stearns on that day and provide time for a more permanent solution to the institution's difficulties. On Sunday March 16, the Federal Reserve extended $29 billion against $30 billion in collateral, again at the primary credit rate of interest, to facilitate the acquisition of Bear Stearns by JPMorgan Chase.[43] The loans to Bear Stearns were the first time the Federal Reserve had used its authority to lend to non-banks since the 1930s.[44, 45, 46]

September 2008 – March 2009

On 16 September 2008, the Federal Reserve provided **American International Group** (AIG) with an $85 billion line of credit secured by all the assets of AIG and its primary non-regulated subsidiaries. The firm was unable to raise funds to post collateral to cover exposures related to declines in the prices of mortgage-related assets, and also faced an imminent downgrade in its credit rating that would have resulted in additional collateral calls on the institution.[47] The loan was extended at Libor plus 850 basis points. On 10 November, "... in order to keep the company strong and facilitate its ability to complete its restructuring successfully, ..." the Federal Reserve restructured the loan, including by lowering the interest rate to Libor plus 300 basis points.[48] AIG was a large insurance company and diversified financial services company with assets as of 20 June 2008 of over $1 trillion. The Federal Reserve determined that the failure of AIG only days after the failure of Lehman Brothers would have severely disrupted financial markets and "materially weakened economic performance".[49] The Federal Reserve was specifically concerned about the risk of contagion from an AIG failure. As described by Chairman Ben Bernanke in testimony before Congress on AIG:

---

[42]   See "Report pursuant to Section 129 of the Emergency Economic Stabilization Act of 2008: Bridge Loan to the Bear Stearns Companies Inc. through JPMorgan Chase Bank, N.A."

[43]   See "Report pursuant to Section 129 of the Emergency Economic Stabilization Act of 2008: Loan to facilitate the acquisition of the Bear Stearns Companies Inc. by JPMorgan Chase & Co."

[44]   That authority is authorised under Section 13(3) of the Federal Reserve Act, and such lending is therefore sometimes called 13(3) lending.

[45]   Although the Term Securities Loan Facility (discussed below) was authorised on 11 March 2008, it was first used on 27 March, after the loan to Bear Stearns.

[46]   On 30 June 2010, $29 billion was outstanding on the loans extended to facilitate the acquisition of Bear Stearns by JPMorgan Chase and the collateral backing the loan had a fair value of $29 billion. Most of the collateral was Federal agency-guaranteed MBS, but over 8% of the securities were rated below investment grade ("Federal Reserve System Monthly Report on Credit and Liquidity Programs and the Balance Sheet" (June 2009)). On 14 June 2012, the Federal Reserve Bank of New York announced that the loan had been repaid in full with interest.

[47]   "Report pursuant to Section 129 of the Emergency Economic Stabilization Act of 2008: Secured Credit Facility Authorized for American International Group, Inc. on September 16, 2008", p 2.

[48]   "Report pursuant to Section 129 of the Emergency Economic Stabilization Act of 2008: Restructuring the Government's Financial Support to the American International Group, Inc. on November 10, 2008", pp 4 and 6.

[49]   "Report pursuant to Section 129 of the Emergency Economic Stabilization Act of 2008: Securities Borrowing Facility for the American International Group, Inc. on October 6, 2008," p 2.

Moreover, as the Lehman case clearly demonstrates, focusing on the direct effects of a default on AIG's counterparties understates the risks to the financial system as a whole. Once begun, a financial crisis can spread unpredictably. For example, Lehman's default on its commercial paper caused a prominent money market mutual fund to "break the buck" and suspend withdrawals, which in turn ignited a general run on prime money market mutual funds, with resulting severe stresses in the commercial paper market. As I mentioned, AIG had about $20 billion in commercial paper outstanding, so its failure would have exacerbated the problems of the money market mutual funds. Another worrisome possibility was that uncertainties about the safety of insurance products could have led to a run on the broader insurance industry by policyholders and creditors. Moreover, it was well known in the market that many major financial institutions had large exposures to AIG. Its failure would likely have led financial market participants to pull back even more from commercial and investment banks, and those institutions perceived as weaker would have faced escalating pressure.[50]

The credit extension to AIG was restructured several times. On 31 March 2010, $15.3 billion of the credit was outstanding to an SPV – Maiden Lane II LLC – backed by assets worth $16.2 billion. The assets were primarily private (non-agency) MBS rated below investment grade. In addition, $17.3 billion was outstanding to another SPV – Maiden Lane III – secured by a range of ABS worth $23.7 billion. Virtually all of those securities – 97% – were rated BB+ or lower. The loans to Maiden Lane II and Maiden Lane III were repaid in full with interest on 1 March 2012 and 14 June 2012, respectively.

HBOS and *Royal Bank of Scotland* (RBS) received ELA by the Bank of England on a large scale at the height of the financial crisis, with an intraday peak of £61.5 billion (Plenderleith (2012)). Plenderleith (2012) describes the Bank of England's ELA as follows: "HBOS first received ELA on 1 October 2008 and at peak on 13 November had drawn £25.4 billion. HBOS made final repayment of the facility on 16 January 2009; RBS first received ELA on 7 October 2008, initially in dollars, but subsequently from 10 October also in sterling. Its use of the dollar facility peaked at $25 billion on 10 October, and of the sterling facility at £29.4 billion on 27 October. RBS made final repayment of ELA on 16 December 2008. ... The sterling ELA took the form of collateral swaps, under which the Bank lent the two banks UK Treasury bills (T-bills) against unsecuritised mortgage and loan assets. The structure was similar in form to the Special Liquidity Scheme (SLS), under which the Bank had been providing liquidity against an extended range of collateral on a market-wide basis since April 2008. The Bank charged a fee of 200 basis points on amounts drawn. The Bank received an indemnity from HM Treasury (HMT) for any additional amounts drawn after 13 October. Before that indemnity was put in place, the full £51.1 billion of the Bank's exposure at that date was not indemnified. Even after the indemnity was in place, the Bank remained unindemnified for £50.9 billion of its peak intraday exposure of £61.5 billion on 17 October. The ELA operation was conducted covertly; it was publicly disclosed on 24 November 2009, just over a year after it was initiated."

---

[50] Testimony of Chairman Ben Bernanke on American International Group before the Committee on Financial Services, US House of Representatives, 24 March 2009.

On 16 October 2008, the Swiss National Bank (SNB) announced that it would finance the transfer of illiquid assets of UBS to an SPV. UBS, one of the two largest Swiss banks, had announced record losses running into billions of Swiss francs, largely attributable to the poor performance of its trading business. In addition, the market's confidence in the big banks had been seriously eroded. After the collapse of Lehman Brothers, confidence weakened even further. As a result, prices for credit default swaps (CDS) increased sharply, share prices plummeted, ratings were downgraded and the big banks' liquidity situation deteriorated (SNB (2009)). The SNB Stabilisation Fund was set up to acquire illiquid assets from UBS up to a maximum amount of $60 billion. The SPV was financed with a maximum of $6 billion equity provided by UBS (taking the first loss position) and a secured long-term loan in an amount not exceeding $54 billion. The SPV paid interest at one-month Libor plus 250 basis points.[51]

On 23 November 2008, the Federal Reserve joined the US Treasury and the Federal Deposit Insurance Corporation (FDIC) in providing **Citigroup** with protection against declines in value on a $306 billion pool of primarily mortgage-related assets.[52] Under the agreement, Citigroup absorbed any initial losses, followed by the Treasury and then the FDIC. If losses exceeded $44 billion, the Federal Reserve would have provided to Citi a non-recourse loan backed by the remaining assets. If the losses continued, Citi could elect to surrender the collateral rather than repay the loan, subject to a 10% loss-sharing agreement.

On 15 January 2009, the Federal Reserve, Treasury and FDIC provided similar protection for **Bank of America** on a $118 billion pool of loans, mortgage-related securities, corporate debt and derivatives. The pool was made up primarily of assets recently acquired by Bank of America in its acquisition of Merrill Lynch. Bank of America had posted material losses on the assets in the fourth quarter of 2008, which had hampered its ability to obtain funding. Further losses "... could have resulted in other financial institutions experiencing similar funding problems, posed risks to financial stability, and increased downside risks to economic growth".[53] If losses on the pool had exceeded $18 billion, the Federal Reserve would have extended to Bank of America a non-recourse loan collateralised by the remaining assets, with the bank obliged to cover 10% of any additional losses.

Neither the Citigroup nor the Bank of America wraps were used, and the institutions paid exit fees to terminate the agreements.

In addition to providing credit to individual non-banking institutions under its emergency lending authority, the Federal Reserve System also provided ELA through the discount window to individual depository institutions that were experiencing financial difficulties. Institutions that are not financially sound do not qualify for the primary credit facility, but may be provided with secondary credit loans. Secondary

---

[51] Subsequently, the amount of UBS assets transferred to the SNB Stabilisation Fund was reduced to $39.1 billion. Greater scope for transferring securitised assets to the banking book, which avoided valuation losses from reporting assets at market prices, allowed UBS to retain part of the assets on its own balance sheet (SNB (2009)).

[52] "Report Pursuant to Section 129 of the Emergency Economic Stabilization Act of 2008: Authorization to Provide Residual Financing to Citigroup, Inc. For a Designated Asset Pool."

[53] "Report Pursuant to Section 129 of the Emergency Economic Stabilization Act of 2008: Authorization to Provide Residual Financing to Bank of America Corporation Relating to a Designated Asset Pool", p 3.

credit loans are available as a bridge to market sources of funds or to facilitate an orderly resolution. The Federal Reserve is subject to legal restrictions on its lending to undercapitalised institutions. While such lending is not prohibited, lending beyond certain time periods – in particular, lending to a critically undercapitalised bank beyond five days – is subject to heightened Congressional scrutiny and subjects the Board to part of any resulting increase in resolution costs. Secondary credit outstanding, which is usually zero, peaked at $985 million on 27 January 2010 (weekly average). The Federal Reserve has not in the past released information about the details on individual discount window borrowings by depository institutions, in part out of concerns that such information increases stigma. However, as required by the Dodd-Frank Act, the Federal Reserve is now publishing with a two-year lag details about all discount window loans including both primary and secondary credit loans made after the law was passed on 21 July 2010.[54]

---

[54] Moreover, on 31 March 2011, in response to a request filed under the Freedom of Information Act, the Federal Reserve released additional information on normal discount window borrowing during the financial crisis.

References

Allen, W and R Moessner (2010): "Central bank co-operation and international liquidity in the financial crisis of 2008–9", *BIS Working Papers*, no 310, May.

Bagehot, W (1873): *Lombard Street: A Description of the Money Market*, London, H S King.

Bank for International Settlements (1974): Communiqué issued by Central Bank Governors of the Group of Ten and Switzerland, 9 September.

———— (1997): *Real-time gross settlement systems: a report prepared by the Committee on Payment and Settlement Systems of the Central Banks of the G10 Countries*, Basel.

———— (2014): *84th Annual Report*, Basel.

Bank of England (2007a): "Liquidity Support Facility for Northern Rock plc", news release, 14 September.

———— (2007b): "Northern Rock plc deposits", news release, 9 October.

Basel Committee on Banking Supervision (2009): "International framework for liquidity risk measurement, standards and monitoring", consultative document.

———— (2010): "Group of Governors and Heads of Supervision announces higher global minimum capital standards", press release, 12 September.

———— (2014): "Results of the Basel III monitoring exercise as of 30 June 2013", 6 March.

Bordo, M (1990): "The lender of last resort: alternative views and historical experience", *Federal Reserve Bank of Richmond Economic Review*, Jan/Feb, pp 18–29.

Borio, C. and W. Nelson (2008), "Monetary operations and the financial turmoil", BIS Quarterly review, March, pp. 31-46.

Carlson, M (2007): "A brief history of the 1987 stock market crash with a discussion of the Federal Reserve response", *Federal Reserve Board Finance and Economics Discussion Series*, no 2007–13.

Carlson, M, B Duygan-Bump and W Nelson (2014): "Why do we need liquidity regulations when we have a central bank?", mimeograph.

Cheun, S., I. Köppen-Mertes and B. Weller (2009): "The collateral frameworks of the Eurosystem, the Federal Reserve system and the Bank of England and the financial market turmoil", ECB Occasional Paper no. 107.

Committee on the Global Financial System (2010a): "The functioning and resilience of cross-border funding markets", *CGFS Papers*, no 37, March.

———— (2010b): "The role of margin requirements and haircuts in procyclicality", *CGFS Papers*, no 36, March.

Corrigan, E (1990): "Statement before U.S. Senate Committee on Banking, Housing and Urban Affairs", Washington DC.

Cour-Thimann, P and B Winkler (2013): "The ECB's non-standard monetary policy measures – the role of institutional factors and financial structure", *ECB Working Paper* no 1528.

Crockett, A (1996): "The theory and practice of financial stability", *De Economist*, vol 144(4), pp 531–68.

Domanski, D (2010): "Exit from unconventional monetary policy measures and the future of central bank operational frameworks", Austrian National Bank Economic Conference, pp 72-83

European Central Bank (2008), "Supplementary six-month longer-term refinancing operations and continuation of the supplementary three-month longer-term refinancing operations", Press release, 28 March.

European Commission (2008): "Proposal for a directive of the European Parliament and of the Council amending directives 2006/48/EC and 2006/49/EC as regards banks affiliated to central institutions, certain own funds items, large exposures, supervisory arrangements, and crisis management".

Financial Services Authority (2009): "Strengthening liquidity standards", Policy Statement 09/16, October.

Fisher, P (2012): "Liquidity support from the Bank of England – the Discount Window Facility", speech at the National Asset-Liability Management global conference, London, 29 March.

Freixas, X, C Giannini, G Hoggarth and F Soussa (1999): "Lender of last resort: a review of the literature", *Bank of England Financial Stability Review*, November, pp 151–67.

Garcia, G and E Plautz (1988): *The Federal Reserve: Lender of Last Resort*, Ballinger, Cambridge, MA.

Geithner, T (2008): "Reducing systemic risk in a dynamic financial system", remarks at the Economic Club of New York, New York City, 9 June.

Goodfriend, M and R King (1988): "Financial deregulation, monetary policy and central banking", *Federal Reserve Bank of Richmond Economic Review*, vol 74, no 3.

Goodhart, C and D Schoenmaker (1995), "Should the Functions of Monetary Policy and Banking Supervision be Separated?", *Oxford Economic Papers*, vol 47, pp 539–60.

Greenspan, A (1988): "Statement and comments of Alan Greenspan, Chairman of the Federal Reserve", in "'Black Monday', The Stock Market Crash of October 19, 1987," U.S. Congress Senate Committee on Banking, Housing, and Urban Affairs Hearing, 100 Congress 1 Session, Washington: Government Printing Office.

HM Treasury (2007): Press notice 107/07, 11 October.

House of Commons Treasury Committee (2008): "The run on the Rock", Fifth Report of Session 2007–08, Volume 1.

King, M (2007): Speech at the Northern Ireland Chamber of Commerce and Industry, Belfast, 9 October.

Madigan, B (2009): "Bagehot's dictum in practice: formulating and implementing policies to combat a financial crisis", speech at the Federal Reserve Bank of Kansas City's Annual Economic Symposium, Jackson Hole, Wyoming, 21 August.

McGuire, P. and G. von Peter (2009): "The US dollar shortage in global banking", BIS Quarterly Review, March.

Moessner, R and W Allen (2010a): "Options for meeting the demand for international liquidity during financial crises", *BIS Quarterly Review*, September.

Moessner, R. and W. Allen (2010b): "Banking crises and the international monetary system in the Great Depression and now", BIS Working Paper no. 333.

Plenderleith, I (2012): "Review of the Bank of England's provision of emergency liquidity assistance in 2008–09", Report presented to the Court of the Bank of England, October.

Pozsar, Z, T Adrian, A Ashcraft and H Boesky (2010): "Shadow banking", *Federal Reserve Bank of New York Staff Reports*, no 458.

Santos, J A C and J Suarez (2014): "The role of liquidity standards in optimal lending of last resort policies", available at SSRN: http://ssrn.com/abstract=2375735.

Schwartz, A (1992): "The misuse of the Fed's discount window", *Federal Reserve Bank of St. Louis Review*, September/October, pp 58–69.

——— (1995): "Systemic risk and the macroeconomy", in G Kaufman (ed), *Banking Financial Markets and Systemic Risk: Research in Financial Services, Private and Public Policy*, vol 7, JAI Press Inc., Hampton, pp 19–30.

Stein, J C (2013): "Liquidity regulation and central banking", remarks at the 2013 Credit Markets Symposium.

Stella, P. (1997), "Do central banks need capital?", IMF Working Paper no. WP/97/83.

Swiss National Bank (2009), Financial Stability Report

Tucker, P (2009): "The repertoire of official sector interventions in the financial system: last resort lending, market-making and capital", presentation at the Bank of Japan 2009 International Conference: Financial System and Monetary Policy: Implementation.

——— (2014): "Regulatory reform, stability, and central banking", Brookings Hutchins Center on Fiscal and Monetary Policy Working Paper.

www.ingramcontent.com/pod-product-compliance
Lightning Source LLC
Chambersburg PA
CBHW080528190526
45169CB00008B/3088